The Young Geographer Investigates

Tropical Forests

Terry Jennings

Oxford University Press

1259

Oxford University Press, Walton Street, Oxford OX2 6DP

Oxford   New York   Toronto
Delhi   Bombay   Calcutta   Madras   Karachi
Petaling Jaya   Singapore   Hong Kong   Tokyo
Nairobi   Dar es Salaam   Cape Town
Melbourne   Auckland

and associated companies in
Berlin   Ibadan

Oxford is a trade mark of Oxford University Press

ISBN 0 19 917074 6 (Paperback)
ISBN 0 19 917080 0 (Hardback)

First published 1986
Reprinted 1988, 1989, 1990

Typeset in Great Britain by
Tradespools Limited, Frome, Somerset
Printed in Hong Kong

Acknowledgements

The publishers would like to thank the following for permission to reproduce transparencies

Aspect Picture Library: p. 26 (top and bottom), p. 29, p. 33 (bottom right), p. 37 (top right), p. 38 (bottom right), p. 40 (top right); A-Z Botanical collection: p. 21 (left and right); Bruce Coleman/Frith: p. 5 (left), B.C./Schultz: p. 5 (top right), B.C./Marigo: p. 5 (bottom left), B.C./Compost: p. 11 (left), p. 14 (inset), B.C./Calhoun: p. 16 (bottom), B.C./Burton: p. 22, B.C./Hinchcliffe: p. 23, B.C./Crichton: p. 24, B.C./Jackson: p. 28 (right); Sally and Richard Greenhill: p. 35 (top); Susan Griggs/Gurney: p. 32 (top left), S.G./REFLEJO: p. 33 (bottom left), p. 39, S.G./Harvey: p. 35 (left), S.G./Woldendorp: p. 37 (left), S.G./Englebert: p. 38 (left); Robert Harding Associates: p. 33 (top left), p. 35 (bottom right); R.H./Ian Griffiths: p. 9 (bottom left); Alan Hutchison Library: p. 13 (bottom left), p. 17 (top), p. 34 (bottom), p. 36 (bottom), p. 38 (top right), A.H./von Puttkamer: p. 27 (top), A.H./Régent: p. 37 (bottom right); Terry Jennings: p.9 (top left); Malaysian High Commission: p. 30; Tony and Marion Morrison: p. 9 (bottom left, top right), p. 14 (top), p. 15 (top right, bottom right), p. 25, p. 27 (left and right), p. 32 (right), p. 33 (top right), p. 40 (bottom right); Oxford Scientific Films/Bernard: Front cover, p. 6, p. 7 (top right, bottom right); p. 10, OSF/Cooke: p. 11 (top right), p. 13 (bottom right), p. 16 (centre), OSF/Dalton: p. 11 (bottom left), p. 12 (left), OSF/Fogden: p. 8, p. 12 (right), p. 16 (top), OSF/Waina Cheng: p. 13 (top left, top right), OSF/Survival Anglia: p. 17 (middle), OSF/Surival Anglia/Lee Lyon: p. 28 (left), OSF/Survival Anglia/Bartlett: p. 32 (bottom left; OUP ©/Mark Mason: p. 35 (inset); Ken Rubeli: p. 31 (top and bottom); Jeffrey Tabberner: P. 34 (top); Timber Research and Development Association: p. 17 (bottom left, centre left, bottom right); Zefa:/Bonath: p.4, Zefa/Halin: p. 15 (left), Zefa/Abril: p.36 (top), Zefa/Mohr: p. 36 (centre).

Illustrations by Norma Burgin, Stephen Cocking, Gary Hincks, Ben Manchipp, Ed McLachlan, Pinpoint Graphics, Tudor Artists, Claire Wright

Contents

Tropical forests

All around the world there are large areas of tropical forest. They are all near the Equator. The Equator is an imaginary line around the middle of the Earth. In places near the Equator the temperatures are high all year long. The only time it gets cooler is at night. There is also a lot of rain all the year round. Because of this, these forests are often called tropical rainforests.

The largest areas of tropical forest are in South America and West Africa. But there are some tropical forests in Indonesia, Malaysia, southern India, Sri Lanka and Pakistan. Smaller pieces also occur in Australia and New Guinea.

Many useful things like rubber, Brazil nuts, bananas, coffee, cocoa and nutmegs come from tropical forest regions. So do some of our most valuable timbers. These include teak, mahogany and rosewood.

A tropical forest in Hawaii

The tropical forests of the Earth

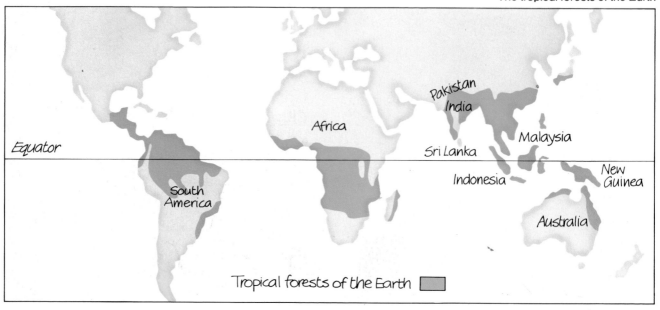

Equator

Pakistan
India
Africa
Sri Lanka
Malaysia
Indonesia
New Guinea
South America
Australia

Tropical forests of the Earth

4

Inside a tropical forest

Tropical forests are sometimes called jungles. This is not a good name to use because not all of these forests are dense. Often they are dense only at the edges or where the forest borders a river or clearing.

The inside of the forest is always dark. This is because the trees keep their leaves all the year round and only a little light reaches the ground. Only a few ferns and other plants can grow under the trees. One of the big differences between tropical forests and forests in the rest of the world is in the huge variety of trees. One hectare of forest in Europe often contains only 10 or 12 kinds of trees. But a hectare of tropical forest may contain 200 kinds of trees.

The trees in a tropical forest are also very large and close together. They are often 60 metres high and have a circumference of more than 5 metres. Because the trees are evergreen, there are always leaves and fruits for animals to eat. And so there are many more kinds of animals, including birds and insects. Altogether, tropical forests are the home for almost half of the different kinds of plants and animals in the world. There are so many kinds of plants and animals in tropical forests that some of them have not even been given names.

Some of the many birds found in tropical forests: *left* pied hornbill; *top right* toucan; *bottom right* vinaceous-breasted parrots.

The parts of a tree

Trees are large, woody plants. They are the world's largest plants. All trees have three main parts. There is a thick woody stem called a trunk. Then there is the crown of the tree, made up of leaves and branches. The very thin branches are called twigs. At certain times of the year there may be buds, flowers or fruit on the twigs.

At the base of the tree are a large number of spreading roots. Some trees have one large root called a tap root. This tap root grows deep into the soil and has smaller roots growing from it. Other trees have many large and small roots. The roots often spread as far underground as the twigs spread in the crown of the tree.

The roots anchor the tree. They stop strong winds blowing the tree over. Roots also take up water and mineral salts from the soil. Tree roots take up huge amounts of water from the soil. In one day, the roots of a large tree may take up well over 200 litres of water from the soil.

A tropical forest tree in Venezuela

The parts of a tree

crown

leaves

twig

branch

trunk

tap root

root

How a tree makes its food

The leaves make food for the tree. To make food, the leaves use the water and mineral salts that the roots take up from the soil. The water and mineral salts travel up the tree to little tubes in the veins of the leaves. Leaves also need sunshine and a gas from the air called carbon dioxide in order to make food. The green substance in tree leaves is called chlorophyll. The green chlorophyll in the leaves uses sunshine to turn the water, carbon dioxide and mineral salts into food. One of the waste products of this process is oxygen. Most trees do not grow well in shady places, because there is not enough sunlight for the leaves to make their food.

In many parts of the world, most of the trees lose all their leaves in winter. These are called deciduous trees. Oak, ash, elm and sycamore are common deciduous trees in Europe. They grow new leaves in the spring.

Some trees keep their leaves in the winter. They are called evergreen trees. Holly, pine, laurel and yew are just a few evergreen trees. Many of the trees in tropical forests are evergreens. The leaves of evergreen trees do not last for ever. They fall off a few at a time throughout the year and are replaced gradually.

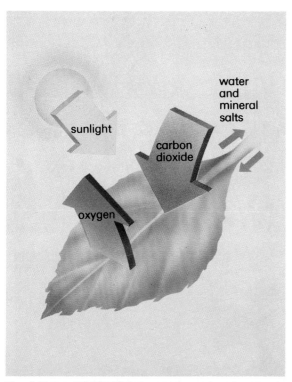

How leaves make food

Deciduous trees in summer and winter

7

Death and decay

When leaves fall from a tree, they lie on the ground in the wind and rain. Gradually they decay or rot away. Earthworms, millipedes and other small animals eat pieces of the dead leaves. Tiny plants such as bacteria and fungi also break up the materials the leaves are made of. Slowly, the leaves are changed to mineral salts in the soil. The mineral salts are used by plants to help make their food. The dead leaves act as natural fertilizers for the living plants. All kinds of plants, including trees, take up the mineral salts from the dead leaves which then help them to grow.

When other parts of a tree fall, including the trunk, branches and twigs, they too decay. They also form mineral salts which trees and other plants can use as food. The same mineral salts are being used over and over again.

In the cooler parts of the world decay takes place slowly. Forests in cooler parts of the world often have a thick layer of dead leaves and branches on the ground. But in the hot, moist tropics, decay occurs quickly. And the leaves and branches which fall from the trees soon rot away. The mineral salts in a tropical forest are used over and over again very quickly.

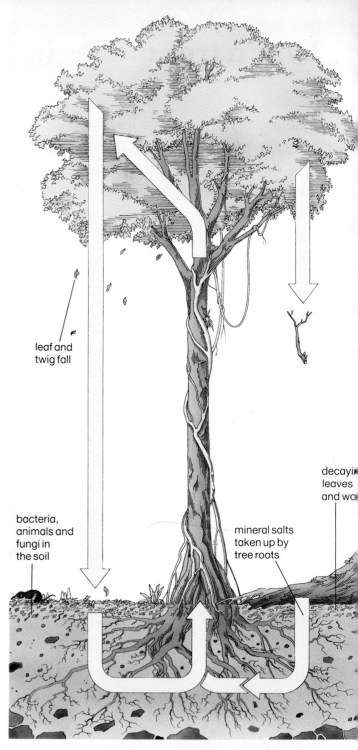

leaf and twig fall

bacteria, animals and fungi in the soil

mineral salts taken up by tree roots

decaying leaves and wo[...]

A millipede feeding on dead leaves

Tropical forest trees

In the cooler parts of the world, winter is a difficult time for trees. The tree roots find it hard to get enough water. The trees stop growing. Often they lose their leaves and rest until the warmer weather returns. But in the tropical forests, the climate is warm and wet all the year round. Most of the tropical forest trees are evergreens. Their leaves are dark green and tough. The leaves usually have a 'drip tip'. This lets the heavy rain run off the leaves. Tropical forest trees can grow and produce flowers and fruit all the year round. Some have flowers and fruit six or more times in a year.

The typical tropical forest tree is more than 40 metres high. It has no branches on most of the trunk. The tree does not branch until near the crown. Often the trees have flowers growing straight out of the trunk or larger branches instead of on twigs.

Many tropical forest trees have roots coming from the trunk above ground. These roots are called buttress roots. They act like the guy-ropes on a tent and stop the tree from falling over. In swampy areas some of the trees have breathing roots. These roots grow above the wet ground and take in the air the tree needs to breathe.

'Drip-tip' on a rubber plant leaf

Tree flowers growing from the trunk

Tropical forest trees have large supporting roots

The layers of the tropical forest

Tropical forests are built up in layers. Here and there huge trees stick up above the rest. Some of these are 60 metres or more in height.

The general level of the forest is made up of trees with rounded crowns. These are about 40 metres high and have upright trunks. They are close enough for their crowns to overlap. Underneath these trees are layers of smaller trees and shrubs. These make use of the little light they can get. Hardly any light reaches the ground. The forest floor is dark and damp. It is mainly mosses and ferns which are able to grow there.

But there are other plants in the tropical forest which grow at several levels. Woody climbing plants called lianes are rooted in the ground. They grow like huge ropes through the canopies of the trees. Having looped their way up one tree, the lianes grow through the crown into another nearby tree. The whole forest is tied together by these woody climbers.

The five layers of a tropical forest

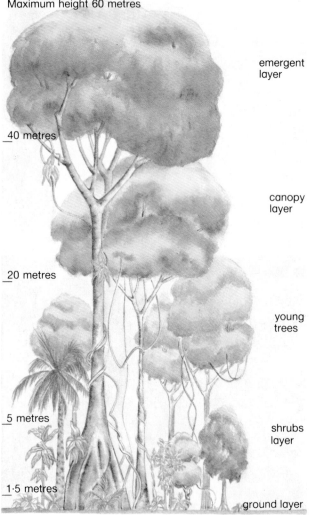

Maximum height 60 metres

40 metres

20 metres

5 metres

1·5 metres

emergent layer

canopy layer

young trees

shrubs layer

ground layer

Lianes in a Venezuelan tropical forest

Plants which depend on others

As well as lianes, a typical forest tree has many other plants growing on it. Many of these are plants called epiphytes. Epiphytes need quite a lot of sunlight. They obtain it by growing high up on the branches of trees. The epiphytes do not use the tree for food. They merely use the tree to help them to get enough sunlight. Among the epiphytes are beautiful orchids. Some of these have special roots to catch and store rainwater.

A few plants grow as parasites. They feed on the tree they are growing on. One parasite is the Malayan plant rafflesia which has brilliant flowers. It grows into the roots of lianes and feeds on their sap.

above A bromeliad epiphyte growing on a tropical forest tree
left A rafflesia flower
below Fallen trees leave gaps in the forest canopy

One day every single tropical forest tree has to die. When it falls, the tree will gradually rot away. Its remains will produce mineral salts which other plants can use. The fallen tree leaves a gap in the canopy of trees. Light can then pass through this gap and reach the ground. Some of the tree seeds on the floor of the forest will grow. Soon a strong young tree will have grown up and closed the gap.

Animal life in the tropical forests

Tropical forests provide animals with food all the year round. There are always flowers, fruits, leaves and nuts for animals to eat. But much of this plant food is high in the trees. Birds are able to fly to reach their food. Many of them have developed special ways of getting their food. Toucans, for example, have long beaks. They can use these to reach the fruits growing on thin branches. Hornbills have similar long beaks. Macaws and parrots have powerful beaks for cracking open nuts and fruit stones. Hummingbirds are able to hover while they sip the nectar from flowers with their long tongues.

Those animals which are not able to fly have to be able to climb to reach food. They are usually small and agile. They often have grasping fingers and a tail which can grip branches. Monkeys have fingers and tails like this. Tree snakes stay on branches by looping their bodies over them.

Because of the thick undergrowth, there are few really large animals living in the forest. They do not have big horns or antlers which would catch on the trees. Most of the tropical forest deer are small. They run through the undergrowth using passages almost like tunnels.

A hummingbird sipping nectar from a flower

Tree snakes live high above the forest floor

Invertebrate animals

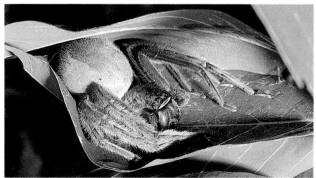

A bird-eating spider in its lair

Tropical forest butterflies searching for moisture

A scorpion in a rainstorm

Leaf-cutter ants at work

Invertebrate animals are those which do not have a skeleton of bone. There are many invertebrate animals in the tropical forests. They grow quickly in the warm conditions. The largest spiders live in holes and under fallen trees. Bird-eating spiders do this. Bird-eating spiders can kill small birds with their poisonous jaws. Scorpions live on the forest floor. They use the sting at the end of their tail to protect themselves. They also use it to kill the small creatures they eat.

There are many large and beautiful butterflies and moths in the tropical forests. Most of them feed on the nectar from flowers. When they rest, some of these butterflies and moths look just like leaves. They are camouflaged. They are almost hidden, and this protects them from being eaten by birds.

Thousands of kinds of ants live on the forest floor. Leaf-cutter ants climb trees and cut off pieces of leaves with their sharp jaws. The leaves are taken back to the ants' nest. There the pieces of leaves are made into little "compost heaps". The ants feed on a fungus which grows on the rotting pieces of leaves.

Forest soils

People used to think tropical forest soils were fertile. This was because so many large plants grew there. We now know that most of the soils in the tropical forests are poor. They are not very fertile. They give poor crops when the forest is cleared. This is because most of the mineral salts are in the trees. The trees also stop the soil from being washed away by the heavy rain.

When the forests are burned down, for a time the ashes act as a fertilizer for the crops. But all the earthworms, termites, ants, bacteria and fungi which turn the dead remains of plants into mineral salts are no longer needed, and they soon disappear. Soon the heavy rain washes away those mineral salts which are left in the soil. Few plants can then grow. And with no plants to protect the soil, the rain washes away the soil itself. And so the area becomes barren. With no trees to soak up the heavy rain, flooding of the lower ground often occurs. Great care has to be taken of the soil when a tropical forest is cleared.

The burning of tropical forest in Brazil

Forest clearance and (inset) the subsequent soil erosion

14

Mangrove swamps

In some places the tropical forests grow right down to the sea. Sometimes the trees can grow in the sea itself. The trees which do this are called mangroves. There are many different kinds of mangrove tree. They all grow where the water is shallow. Some mangroves are quite large trees, up to 30 metres high. They are able to grow in the water because they have special breathing roots.

Mangrove trees also have unusual seeds. The seeds start to grow while they are still on the tree. When the seed has a long root growing from it, it falls from the tree. The seed floats away. If it is washed up on the shore, the root sticks in the mud. The leaves are then able to grow from the seed above the level of the water.

Mangrove trees help to build up the coast. Mud and pieces of dead plants collect in the tangled roots of the mangrove trees. Gradually the level of the mud is raised above the water. Then new dry land is formed. Mangrove trees are the homes for many wild creatures including otters, turtles, crabs and some crocodiles and birds. They also provide firewood and cattle food.

A mangrove swamp in Venezuela

Roots growing from mangrove seeds

A fiddler crab in a Columbian mangrove swamp

Survival in the forest

Tropical forests are difficult places for people to live in. They can be dangerous. Crocodiles and alligators live in the swamps and rivers. There are poisonous snakes and scorpions. Many of the plants, too, are poisonous. Leeches drop from the trees on to people below. There are also leeches in the water. These suck the blood of anyone they can fix themselves to.

Swarms of mosquitoes breed in the swamps and marshes. They carry deadly diseases such as malaria and yellow fever. When the Panama Canal was being dug through the swampy tropical forests of Central America, thousands of workmen died. They died from malaria and yellow fever spread by mosquitoes.

But the native people who live in tropical forests know which plants they can eat. They know which snakes are poisonous. They also know which plants they can use to

A poisonous frog in the South American tropical forest

A mosquito taking a meal of human blood

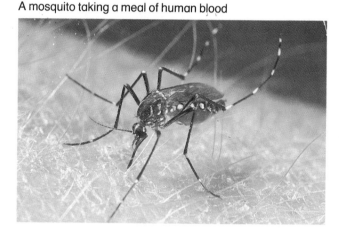

cure their illnesses or to heal their wounds. The native people are experts at living in these difficult and dangerous places.

American alligator

Timber

Only a little of our timber comes from tropical forests. This is in spite of the fact that these forests contain many valuable timber trees. One of the problems is that the valuable trees do not all grow together. Mahogany trees, for example, are widely scattered in the forest. Thus the forester's first problem is to find his tree.

Then it is difficult to cut down the trees. The base of the tree may have buttress roots growing around it. This means that the tree has to be cut where the trunk narrows above these roots. Often this is 3 metres or more above the ground. Platforms have to be built for the foresters to stand on to fell the trees. All the creepers and lianes may stop the cut tree from falling.

Moving the cut tree is another problem. Usually a rough roadway has to be built before the huge logs can be dragged out of the forest. Sometimes the trees can be floated away down a river. Unfortunately many of the trees are too heavy to float. It is also difficult to find workers to carry out this hard work in the hot, wet climate.

Foresters building a platform around a tree

Carrying teak logs in India

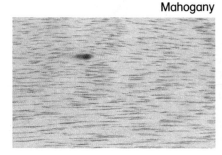

Mahogany

Teak

Iroko

Do you remember?

1 Whereabouts on the Earth are the tropical forests?

2 Name four useful things we get from tropical forests.

3 What are two other names that are often given to tropical forests?

4 Which would contain the most kinds of trees, a hectare of tropical forest or a hectare of forest in the rest of the world?

5 Why are there so many kinds of animals in tropical forests?

6 What are the three main parts of a tree?

7 How do the roots help a tree?

8 What do the leaves of a tree do?

9 Why do most trees not grow well in shady places?

10 What is a deciduous tree?

11 What happens to the parts of a tree which die and fall to the ground?

12 Why do the animals living in tropical forests not have large antlers or horns?

13 What are buttress roots?

14 What are the woody climbing plants called which grow in tropical forests?

15 What are epiphytes?

16 What do we call a plant which gets its food from the tree it grows on?

17 What do the leaves of many tropical forest trees have to let water run off them?

18 What are invertebrate animals?

19 What do scorpions use their stings for?

20 Why did people once think tropical forest soils were fertile?

21 When tropical forests are burned down, why do crops grow well for a year or two?

22 With no plants to protect the soil, what does the rain water do after a forest has been cleared?

23 What are the roots of a mangrove tree like?

24 Where does a mangrove seed start to grow?

25 How do mangrove trees help to build up the coast?

26 What do leeches feed on?

27 Name two diseases spread by mosquitoes.

28 Name two other dangerous animals which are found in tropical forests.

29 Why is it often difficult to cut down tropical forest trees for their timber?

30 Name two valuable timbers which come from tropical forest trees.

Things to do

1 Make a collage Collect pictures of tropical forest plants and animals. Stick your pictures on a large sheet of paper to make one large picture or collage that shows a variety of scenes in a tropical forest.

2 Foods from tropical forests
Many of the foods we buy in the shops are sold in cans, packets, bottles or jars. The labels on them not only tell us what is inside the container, they often tell us the name of the country where the food was grown.

Obtain a small map of the world and stick it in the centre of a large sheet of paper or card. Around the edges of the sheet of paper or card, stick the labels or packet fronts of foods that were grown in tropical forest areas of the world. The foods mentioned on page 4 are some to be going on with. For each label put a pin in the country it came from. Then join the label to the pin by a length of thread. Sellotape the end of the thread on to the label.

3 How many kinds of trees are there? In a hectare of tropical forest there may be 200 different kinds of trees. How many kinds of trees are there in a wood or forest near to where you live? Try to make a list of the different kinds of trees. Use a book to help you to identify them. If there are any trees which you cannot identify, it does not really matter. You can tell by the leaves whether or not the tree is of a different kind from others you do know.

A hectare of land measures approximately 100 x 100 metres

A hectare of temperate forest

A hectare of tropical forest

4 Measure the height of some trees

Find a stick which is one metre long. Put that stick in the ground under the tree you wish to measure. Now stand far enough away so that you can see both the stick and the top of the tree.

Hold a pencil at arm's length and move your thumb until the piece of pencil you have uncovered seems to be the same height as your stick. Now see how many times that same piece of pencil goes into the height of the tree.

Suppose the piece of pencil goes into the tree 15 times, then your tree is 15 metres high.

Use a tape measure or a piece of string and a ruler to measure how far it is round the trunk of the tree. We call this distance the girth of the tree.

Can you find a way to measure how far the branches spread in all directions without climbing the tree?

Which is the tallest tree you can find? How tall is it? Which tree has the biggest girth and the biggest spread of branches? How old do you think each tree is?

5 Measuring the height of tall trees

Here is a way of measuring the height of a tall tree. Take a large 45° set-square. Find a place where you can just see the top of the tree while you look along the longest side of the set-square. Keep one of the other sides horizontal as shown in the picture. The height of the tree will be the same as your distance from the tree, plus your own height. What is the tallest tree you can find? How much shorter is it than the taller tropical forest trees? Make a table of your results.

6 Tree leaves In tropical forests, most of the trees are evergreens. Make a collection of tree leaves. Divide your collection into two. In one part put evergreen tree leaves. In the other put deciduous tree leaves. Look at the leaves carefully. Use a hand lens or magnifying glass to help you to see better. What differences can you see between the two types of leaves? What similarities are there?

7 House plants Many of the plants kept indoors for decoration come from tropical forests. Two of these are the rubber plant (it is not the same plant as the one from which rubber is made), and monstera.

Look at these and some other house plants carefully. Try to find out where they came from originally. Ask permission to stand one of these plants outside on a warm, rainy day. Or perhaps you could spray the plant with water. Watch how the water runs off the leaf. Is the leaf easily wetted?

8 Where does the water go which a plant takes up? Obtain a potted plant – a geranium is ideal – or a young tree in a pot. Water the soil or compost in the pot. Then enclose the plant in a polythene bag. Choose a polythene bag which has no holes in it. Tie the opening of the bag around the stem of the plant.

Stand the plant on a sunny windowsill. Look at the inside of the polythene bag after a day or so. What do you see?

Often clouds form over the trees in a tropical forest during the daytime. Why do you think this is?

9 How fast do leaves decay?

Which tree leaves decay fastest? You will need some tree leaves of different kinds and some flower pots, yoghurt pots or margarine tubs containing moist garden soil.

Bury one leaf of each kind just under the surface of the soil in each pot. Label the pots with the names of the tree leaves in them. Put the pots on a warm windowsill and keep the soil moist. Every two weeks look at the leaves to see how much has decayed away. Then carefully bury the leaves again. Do some of the leaves decay faster than others?

Put some more leaves in pots of soil. This time use leaves which are all of the same kind. Put some of the pots on a warm windowsill. Put the others in a cool place – a refrigerator would be ideal. Which leaves decay the fastest? Where would you expect tree leaves to decay the fastest, in the tropics or in the cooler parts of the world?

Try tying small labels on to some dead tree leaves. Tie each leaf to a little stick in the flower border. Look at the leaves every week and see how fast they decay away. Are any of the leaves eaten by animals? Can you find out what kinds of animals eat the leaves? Which kinds of leaves are eaten most?

10 Gnats and mosquitoes

As we have seen, mosquitoes are feared in the tropical forests of the world because of the diseases they can carry. Happily in the cooler parts of the world gnats and mosquitoes (they are the same thing) do not carry diseases.

During the summer, look on the surface of still water for gnat or mosquito larvae. They are easily reared to the adult insects in jam-jars containing pond water, river water or the stale water from a vase of flowers. Keep the jars out of doors.

Use a magnifying glass or hand lens to study the different stages in the life of a gnat or mosquito. Draw them in your notebook.

Mosquito larvae

11 Ants and food Ants are common almost anywhere. But they are particularly abundant in tropical forests. Find out what kinds of foods the ants in your garden or school grounds like best.

Put a tiny piece of meat or biscuit near an ants' nest. See how many ants come to the food. Do they pull the food to the nest? Now put down another piece of meat or biscuit twice as big as the first piece. Do twice as many ants arrive to pull it into the nest?

Next put down four or five clean milk bottle tops or crown bottle caps near the ants' nest. Put a little jam in one, a little sugar in another, a little marmalade in another, a few biscuit or bread crumbs in the next, and so on. Which bottle top do the ants go to first? Which bottle top do the most ants go to? Do they take any of the foods to the nest?

Now try the experiment with other kinds of foods.

Ants

12 Find out about the content of soil The soil in forests usually contains a lot of a material called humus. Humus is the decaying remains of dead plants and animals. It is the humus in the soil which breaks down to form mineral salts.

Find out more about the content of soil. Put a handful of garden soil in a jar with straight sides. A clear-glass coffee jar is a good one to use. Then pour in water until the jar is about three-quarters full.

Put the lid on the jar and shake it really hard. As soon as you have stopped shaking it, put the jar on a table or windowsill to see how the soil settles.

How long does it take for the water to clear? Can you see layers of different sized pieces? How many layers can you see?

Which layer has the largest pieces? Which layer has the smallest pieces? Measure the thickness of each of the layers.

Are there any little pieces of humus floating on top of the water? These usually look black.

Do the same thing with soils from other places. Make sure you try a soil from under a wood, forest or large tree. If you always use the same kind of jar you can make a table to compare the thicknesses and colours of the different layers in the different soils.

You could also make drawings of the jars containing each of the different soils.

13 Make a collection of timbers Make a collection of small pieces of the timbers that come from tropical forest trees. A carpenter might be able to help you to obtain offcuts of these. Label your collection. Try to find out what each of these timbers is used for. Why are these timbers better for these purposes than timbers from trees that grow elsewhere in the world?

14 Collect pictures Collect pictures of animals and plants of the tropical forest. Make a scrapbook or wall chart of them. Write a sentence or two about each picture.

Things to find out

1 Look at a map of the world which shows the distribution of tropical forests. Roughly what is the greatest distance tropical forests occur north or south of the Equator? Why are there no tropical forests in East Africa or down the western side of South America, even in those places which are on the Equator?

2 Why are the temperatures near the Equator higher than those towards the polar regions? Why are the days all about the same length throughout the year?

3 The tropical forest areas receive more than 200 centimetres of rain a year. What is the wettest part of your country? Why does tropical forest not occur there?

4 Study your atlas. How many continents can you find which contain a large area of tropical forest? Name a country in each of these continents which contains a tropical forest.

5 Are the forests which grow on mountains near the Equator the same as those which grow on the lower-lying land?

6 Why do so few people live in the tropical forests?

7 Through which of the countries of Africa with tropical forest does the Equator pass?

8 Why are rivers more likely to flood if forests growing nearby are cut down?

9 Mineral salts are vital to the growth of plants. In a tropical forest, most of the mineral salts are in the trees. They only go into the soil when the trees die. When farmers send crops to market, they are sending away mineral salts that would have gone into the soil if the crop plants had died and decayed where they were growing. How do farmers put mineral salts back into the soil to make up for those which have been lost?

10 Places where collections of living plants are kept are called botanical gardens. If there is a botanical garden near where you live visit it. What does it feel like to be in one of the greenhouses where tropical forest plants are grown? What is done to make the conditions inside the greenhouse like that? What plants are grown in the tropical forest greenhouses?

11 Choose an animal which lives in one of the tropical forests. Find out all you can about it. How is it able to survive in the forest? Collect as many pictures as you can of your chosen animal. Make a book about your animal.

The Amazon forest

The Amazon forest is in South America. It is the largest tropical forest in the world. It is roughly ten times the size of England. The Amazon forest covers a huge lowland area drained by the River Amazon and its tributaries.

Because the Amazon forest lies across the Equator, the midday sun is overhead throughout the year. The daytime temperatures are always high. The average temperature is about 25°C. There are more than 200 centimetres of rain a year.

Each day in the forest is the same. The sun rises at about 6 am. The early morning mists soon disappear. As the sun gets higher in the sky the temperature rises. A lot of water evaporates from the rivers and also from the trees. As the warm, moist air rises, it cools. The invisible water vapour in the air cools to form huge clouds. By the afternoon there is usually a heavy rainstorm, often with

Rainclouds gathering over the Amazon forest

thunder and lightning. The clouds then break up. At about 6 pm the sun sets and the cooler night begins. There are no summer and winter seasons as we know them.

The Amazon Forest and Equator

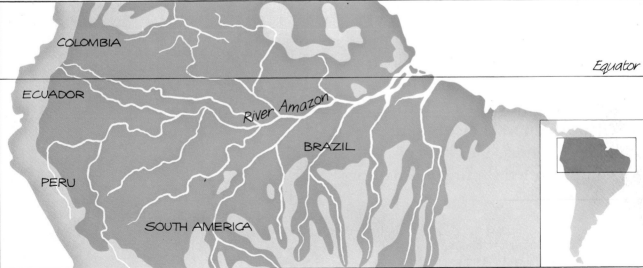

Shifting cultivation

The Waura people live in the Amazon forest. They are one of the tribes of Amazon Indians. The Waura get everything they need from the forest. They hunt animals with blowpipes and poisoned darts. They collect fruits and other parts of plants to eat from the forest. The Waura also carry out a simple kind of farming. This means they can live in one place for a longer period.

In order to grow their crops, the Waura clear a space in the forest. At one side of the clearing the Waura build large huts. These are made from wood and thatched with leaves. Each house is large enough for three or four families.

The crops grow quickly in the warm, moist ground. But only enough of the crop plants are harvested for each meal. It is impossible to store food in this hot, wet climate. In two or three years the crops no longer grow well. The heavy rain has washed away the mineral salts from the soil. A new clearing is made nearby in the forest. Eventually the clearing being used lies a long way from the village. Then the Waura must move to a new area. They make another clearing and build new homes. This kind of farming is called shifting cultivation.

top Waura man preparing his blowpipe
right Clearing the trees and undergrowth to grow crops

The destruction of the Amazon forest

Making a road through the Amazon Forest

In the past few years, over 10 000 kilometres of road have been driven through the Amazon forest. This is so that the forest can be cleared and used for other things. Large areas have been burned. Huge farms have been made in place of the forest. Millions of cattle graze the new land.

Big pieces of the tropical forest have been replaced by faster-growing foreign trees. These are grown for wood pulp which is used to make paper and rayon. The Brazilian government has resettled over a million people from poorer parts of the country. Many of these are farmers. Some grow mainly food for themselves. Others grow crops of coffee, cocoa, palm oil and soya beans to sell. Some of the forest has been cleared so that oil and valuable minerals can be mined.

It is believed that one-fifth of the Amazon forest has already been cleared. At the present rate there will be none left in 25 to 30 years. The Amazon Indians, animals and birds will have nowhere to live.

The farming of cattle on cleared rainforest land

Amazon rainforest cleared for cultivation

The Congo forests

The largest tropical forest in Africa is in the basin of the River Congo. This whole area was once a huge shallow lake. The Congo forests contain more kinds of plants and animals than any other part of Africa. This is the home of the gorilla, chimpanzee and many other kinds of apes and monkeys.

Races of small people, or pygmies, live in parts of the forest. But much of the original tropical forest has been cleared. Some of the forest has been cleared to obtain valuable timbers like mahogany and iroko. The less valuable timber is used locally for building or firewood. Some of the timber is made into plywood or chipboard. The trees are being cut down faster than new ones can grow.

Large areas of the forest have been cleared so that huge fields of oil palm, rubber, bananas and cotton can be planted. Some of the forest has been cleared to obtain oil and minerals.

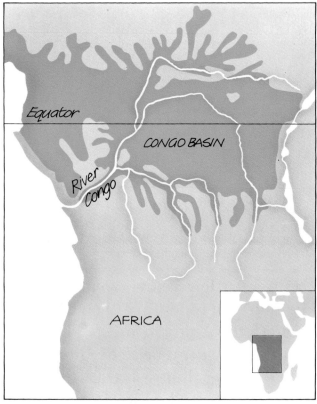

The Congo Forest in West Africa

Some has gone to make room for houses. Parts of the Congo forest have been set aside as national parks or nature reserves. But much of the forest is under threat.

A gorilla in the swamps

Chimpanzees

The smallest people in the world

A Bambuti tribal dance

In the tropical forests of the Congo live the smallest people in the world. These pygmy people are called the Bambuti. The average height of the men is 1.3 metres. The women are even smaller.

The Bambuti live in tribes made up of a few dozen people. They move through the forest, often following a herd of elephants or other animals. They hunt these with bows and arrows and spears. At night the Bambuti make temporary shelters for their families. Thin sticks are stuck in the ground so that they form a circle. Then the ends of the sticks are bent over and tied in the middle. This framework is covered with large leaves to keep out the rain. The family's food is prepared and cooked outside the shelter.

The Bambuti have to exchange with nearby tribes for the other things they need like salt and maize. They exchange ivory, or honey from wild bees, for the salt and maize they need. When they have finished working the Bambuti enjoy music and dancing. In all there are about 30 000 of these pygmy people in the Congo basin. Once there were many more. At one time it is believed that these small people were found over much of Africa.

The Negrito people of Malaysia

The Malay peninsula is a mountainous area. It is covered in dense tropical forest. This forest is the home of the Negrito people. The Negritos are a race of small people. They live in family groups of between about 10 and 60 people.

The Negritos do not grow crops or keep animals. All their food and other needs come from the forest. They collect fruits, roots, nuts and shoots to eat. The Negritos use snares and poisoned arrows to catch monkeys, rats, squirrels, lizards and birds for meat. Fish are caught in the rivers with spears.

As soon as they have eaten all the food in one area, the Negritos move on. A new camp site is chosen. They sleep in caves, beneath rock overhangs and in hollow trees. Sometimes raised shelters are built.

Each of these is a framework of thin branches thatched with leaves. The only furniture is a wooden platform to sleep on. In less than a week the camp is left. The group moves on to a new one. The Negritos do not move just anywhere. Each tribe stays within its own territory which is about 50 square kilometres in area.

A Negrito family

The Senoi people of Malaysia

Unlike the Negrito people, the Senoi of Malaysia are farmers. They live in a lonely mountainous area. Each group has a long bamboo house and several smaller huts.

Many of the Senoi carry out shifting cultivation. In the driest part of the year they cut down and burn a small area of forest. The wood ash acts as a fertilizer. The Senoi then plant crops of bananas, rice, tapioca and millet in the clearing. They also fish and hunt using blowpipes and poison darts, and they collect wild fruits from the forest. The Senoi farmers do not have any food to sell. They produce just enough food to live on. After 2 or 3 years the heavy rains have washed the mineral salts out of the soil. Then the people leave the clearing and make a new one.

below A Senoi family   *right* Senoi children

This kind of shifting cultivation works well as long as there are not too many people in the forest area. But the number of people in Malaysia is increasing. And the land is being taken over by wealthy farmers who want to grow crops to sell. Large areas of land are being cleared and planted with rice, and rubber trees. Soon there will not be enough land for the Senoi's shifting cultivation. The Senoi will then have to start a new way of life.

The Australian tropical forests

Australia has only small patches of tropical forest left. The largest remaining areas are in the north-eastern corner of Queensland. Parts of these have been set aside as nature reserves. These tropical forests contain many eucalyptus trees. Eucalyptus trees are often called gum trees. In the warm, wet forests, eucalyptus trees grow very tall. One kind can grow to be 100 metres high. The forests include some valuable timber trees.

Growing amongst the eucalyptus trees are strangler fig plants. The seeds of these plants are scattered by birds and flying foxes. The seeds may lodge in the branches of a tree, where they grow. The roots of the fig wind around the tree so much that the tree dies. The fig then grows in the space

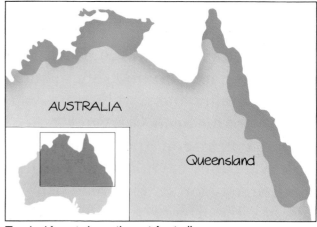

Tropical forests in north-east Australia

left by the tree it has killed.

The Australian tropical forests are homes for several kinds of kangaroos and wallabies. Duck-billed platypuses live there, too. Where the forest has been cleared, sugar cane and tropical fruits are grown. These crops grow rapidly in the warm, moist climate. Some cattle are also kept for their meat and milk.

A eucalyptus forest

A duck-billed platypus

The strangler fig

Plantations

In most parts of the world, large areas of tropical forest have been cleared to make way for huge farms. These huge farms are called plantations. Plantations grow one of the tropical crops. There are many of these including sugar, oil palm, cocoa, coffee, rubber, bananas, pineapples, cotton and rice. There are also a few plantations of timber trees such as teak. All of these crops are sold to countries overseas.

A lot of workers are needed on the plantations. Most of these workers have to be brought in from outside the forest areas. At one time many of the plantation workers were slaves. Special villages have to be built where the plantation workers can live.

Banana plant

above Harvesting pineapples
left A pineapple plantation
below left An irrigation canal on a banana plantation

The plants grown on the plantations are no longer the same as those which grow wild. They have been changed by scientists. The banana plant, for example, no longer produces seeds. New banana plants are grown from pieces cut off the old plants.

A lot of fertilizers have to be used on the plantations. This is because the soil is poor. With vast areas given over to one crop, pests and diseases can spread quickly. Chemicals have to be used to kill the weeds and pests.

Rubber trees

Natural rubber is made from latex. This milky white juice comes from the rubber tree. Rubber trees grow wild in the Amazon forests. The rubber trees are widely scattered there. Because the trees are hard to find, it is expensive to collect enough latex to make rubber.

In 1876 rubber tree seeds were taken from South America to London. Little trees were grown from the seeds. These trees were sent to other countries with the same hot, wet climate as the Amazon forests. Today plantations of rubber trees are grown in several countries. They can be found in Indonesia, Malaysia, Thailand, Sri Lanka and parts of West Africa.

Nowadays the rubber tree seeds are planted in special nurseries. As the seedlings grow they are shaded from the hot sun. When they are

Latex is the milky white juice obtained from rubber trees

large enough, the young rubber trees are planted out in rows. Other crops are planted between the rubber trees. These plants help to keep the soil moist by shading it from the sun. They also help to keep down the weeds and stop the soil from being washed or blown away. After about 5 years the rubber trees are 9 metres high. They are ready to give the latex from which rubber is made.

A nursery of rubber tree seedlings in Nigeria

34

Making rubber

The person who collects the latex is called a tapper. He or she starts work early in the morning. The tapper uses a sharp knife to make a sloping cut half way round the tree. At the lower end of the cut, the tapper hangs a cup. Very, very slowly latex trickles from under the bark of the tree into the cup. Every two or three days the latex from each tree is collected. One person may collect the latex from 300 to 500 trees in a day.

The latex is taken by lorry to the factory. At the factory, acid is added to the latex. This separates the solid rubber from the liquid part. The rubber is rolled into flat sheets. When the sheets are dry they are baled up and sent to those countries where rubber is used.

above A rubber tapper at work

below left Sheets of rubber hanging up to dry
below Blocks of raw rubber, and *inset* rubber goods

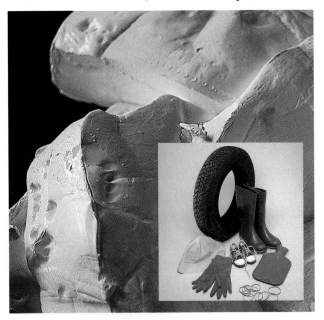

Rubber is used for tyres, hot water bottles, wellington boots, gym shoes, balls, hoses and many other things. Nowadays we use so much rubber that rubber trees cannot produce enough. A lot of rubber is now made from oil. For some things this artificial or synthetic rubber is better than natural rubber.

Cacao trees

Cacao trees have large seed pods. Each pod is about 25 centimetres long. Inside the pods are seeds, called beans. It is from these beans that chocolate and cocoa are made.

Like rubber trees, cacao trees grow wild in the Amazon forests. But now they are planted in other tropical areas. Mostly they are grown in Brazil and Ecuador in South America, and in parts of West Africa. In South America cacao is grown in large plantations. But in West Africa it is grown on smaller plots. In West Africa some of the taller trees are left when the forest is cleared. These shade the cacao trees. They also shelter the cacao trees from the strong winds.

The cacao trees begin to flower and bear pods when they are 4 to 5 years old. When the pods are ripe they are cut off with a large knife. The pods are split open and the cacao beans are scraped out. The beans are piled into heaps and covered with leaves. This is so that the pulp around the beans rots away. Then the beans are dried in the sun. When thoroughly dry, the beans are put into sacks and taken to the coast. Ships take the beans to Europe, America and other countries where cocoa and chocolate are made.

top right Harvesting cacao pods in Brazil

centre right Cacao beans inside the pod

bottom right Cacao beans drying in the Nigerian sun

Oil palms

The oil palm tree grows wild in the tropical forests of West Africa. It is now grown in plantations in West Africa, Malaysia and Indonesia. The oil palm grows tall and straight. It has no branches. But a mass of large, feathery leaves grow from the top.

The oil palm bears its bright red fruit in bunches. Each bunch may weigh 15 to 20 kilogrammes. Because of the hot, wet climate, an oil palm tree grows quickly. It may flower and fruit between 12 and 20 times a year. The fruits are cut off with a sharp knife on the end of a long pole.

The fruits are taken to the factory. There they are split open. Inside each fruit is a hard seed. This is surrounded by a mass of fibrous tissues. Both the seeds and fibrous tissue contain oil. This oil is collected. It is used to make soap, margarine and candles. Oil palm fruits are also used by the natives for cooking and lighting.

Bunches of oil palm fruits

Ripe fruits

Plantation of young oil palm trees

Coffee trees

Picking coffee in Columbia

Coffee berries from Kenya

Coffee beans being dried in the sun

Coffee trees came originally from Africa. Now plantations of them are grown in several places including the tropical forest areas of Brazil and West Africa. The coffee trees are grown from seed in a nursery. After 18 months or so the young trees are planted out in rows. Taller trees are planted between the coffee trees. This is to give the coffee trees the shade they need. Usually the coffee trees are grown on large plantations which contain thousands of trees.

When the coffee trees are 4 years old, they produce small berries. As these turn cherry-red, they are ready for picking. The berries are picked by

hand. Inside each small red berry are two green seeds. These are the coffee 'beans'.

The beans are separated from the fleshy parts of the berry. First the coffee berries are spread out on concrete floors painted black so that they warm up in the sun. After a few days the berries are dry. The shrivelled berries are then opened to reach the coffee beans. Sometimes this is done by machine but mostly it is done by hand. The coffee beans are then dried, sorted and packed in sacks. They are shipped to the places where the beans are roasted ready for making coffee.

Sugar cane

Sugar cane is the main plant grown on the land cleared from tropical forests in the West Indies. It is also grown in Australia, Brazil, India, Cuba and parts of the southern United States. Sugar cane is a very large member of the grass family. Some sugar canes grow to be over 6 metres tall. The stems may be 5 centimetres in diameter at their bases.

The farmers who live on the plantations plant the sugar canes in the early spring. But they do not replant the cane every year, for new plants will grow from the stalks of the old sugar cane. Usually the sugar cane is replanted every three or four years. The summer and autumn is spent keeping the sugar cane free from weeds. Only a few workers are needed for this job.

But the harvest is a busy time. In the winter and spring thousands of people work in the cane fields. Sometimes the cane fields are burned to drive off snakes and scorpions. The cane is cut by hand in many places. But machines are being used more and more. The cut cane is then quickly taken to the mill. At the mill the cane is cut into pieces. These are then crushed by huge rollers to squeeze out the juice. Finally the juice is boiled until it forms crystals of sugar.

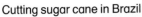
Cutting sugar cane in Brazil

The disappearing forests

The world's tropical forests are in great danger. They are being cleared at a faster rate than ever before. In the time it takes you to read this sentence, between 20 and 40 hectares of tropical forest will have been damaged or destroyed.

The forests are being cleared to produce timber and firewood and also in order to grow food. They are being cleared to make room for houses, roads, farms and factories. Parts of the forest are being cut down to obtain oil and valuable minerals.

If people go on cutting down the forest at this rate, by the year 2000 only West Africa and the Amazon basin will have any tropical forest left. The groups of people who live in the forests will have lost their homes. Or they will have had to change their way of life. Some of the world's most interesting and beautiful plants and animals will have become extinct. Animals like the sloth, tiger, gorilla, jaguar, orang-utan and birds of paradise will have become extinct.

The greater bird of paradise

Trees purify the air we need to breathe. If too many trees are chopped down, the air in the forest changes. And this affects the weather. Some scientists are worried that if we cut down the big tropical forests, the whole of the world's climate may change.

A female three-toed sloth from Panama

A jaguar from Brazil

Do you remember?

1 On which continent is the Amazon forest?

2 What is the weather like each day in the Amazon forest?

3 What do the Waura people use to hunt animals?

4 How many Waura families live in one of their huts?

5 Why do the Waura only harvest enough food for one meal at a time?

6 What is meant by shifting cultivation?

7 Give three reasons why the Amazon forest is being cleared.

8 How much of the Amazon forest has been clearly already?

9 Where is the largest tropical forest in Africa?

10 What is the name usually given to tribes of very small people?

11 Where do the Bambuti people sleep at night?

12 Where do the Negrito people live?

13 Name two of the crops grown by the Senoi people.

14 Why are the Senoi people finding it difficult to carry out their shifting cultivation?

15 Which trees are common in the tropical forests of Australia?

16 Name two of the animals which live in the tropical forests of Australia.

17 What is a plantation?

18 How are new banana plants obtained?

19 Name three of the countries where rubber trees are grown.

20 What is latex?

21 How is latex obtained from the rubber tree?

22 What is done to latex to obtain rubber?

23 Where do cacao trees grow wild?

24 What is inside the pods of the cacao tree?

25 What two things are made from the seed pods of the cacao tree?

26 What is palm oil used for?

27 Why are taller trees planted between rows of coffee trees?

28 What is inside each berry from a coffee tree?

29 What kind of plant is sugar cane?

30 What is done to get sugar from the pieces of sugar cane?

Things to do

1 Grow some tropical forest plants Did you know that you can grow some tropical forest plants wherever you live? Of course the plants have to be kept indoors or in a greenhouse.

Fig seeds are easy to grow. Scoop out the seeds from a dried fig and soak them in a cup of water to remove the sugary flesh. Spread the seeds on clean newspaper until they are dry. Then sprinkle the dried seeds on to the surface of a pot of moist compost. Cover the seeds thinly with some more compost. Stand the pot in a warm cupboard – an airing cupboard is ideal – until the first shoots appear. Then move the pot to a sunny windowsill. Keep the compost moist but not wet. Later, transplant the seedlings separately to small pots.

Plant the nuts about 2 or 3 centimetres deep in groups in a large flowerpot containing moist compost. Cover the pot with a polythene bag for 2 to 3 weeks. Once the nuts show signs of sprouting, move them to a warm, sunny windowsill. Thin the seedlings out to about three or four to a large pot. Keep the compost moist but not soaking wet. You may not be able to get your peanut plants to produce ripe underground nuts, but they will soon grow into attractive house plants.

If you can obtain some *unroasted* coffee beans from a grocer who roasts and grinds his own beans, try to grow them. Plant the beans about 2 centimetres deep in small pots of moist compost. Cover the pots with polythene bags and keep them in a warm

Peanuts or groundnuts are in fact not nuts but relatives of peas and beans. They need a good deal of warmth if they are to grow quickly and healthily. You can plant either shelled nuts or those still in their shells. Do not use roasted or salted nuts, though, and avoid any nuts which show signs of damage.

place (as near to 27°C as you can). When the first shoots appear, move the pots to a warm, sunny windowsill.

Other tropical and sub-tropical plants you might try to grow from seeds or pips include avocados, pomegranates, dates, oranges, lemons, grapefruit, lychees and peaches.

42

2 Growing pineapple tops

Pineapples are grown in several tropical forests areas. It is possible to grow the spiky leaves on the top of a pineapple fruit as a pot plant. The best tops are those which are fresh and green.

Cut off the tip with about 1 centimetre of the fruit attached. Leave to it dry overnight. The next morning scrape away any of the flesh which is still soft and moist. Leave the central part untouched. If you have some, lightly sprinkle the base of the pineapple top with a hormone rooting powder. Then place it in a flowerpot containing moist compost with a layer of crocks or pebbles over the bottom.

Cover the pineapple top and pot with a large polythene bag and stand it on a warm, sunny windowsill. Remove the bag when new leaves start to appear in the centre of the pineapple top.

Pineapple tops have been known to produce fruit of their own. Even if yours does not, you will have an interesting and attractive plant.

3 A model pygmy village

Look at the picture of a pygmy village on page 29. Make a model of a pygmy village set in a forest clearing. Use drinking straws, clay, plasticine, twigs, leaves and any other materials you can find.

4 Tropical fruits on a skewer

This is a refreshing dessert which makes an excellent finish to a meal. Many different fruits can be used, but they must be ripe. Some you might choose include mango, melon, pineapple, banana, kiwi fruits, paw paw and peaches.

Peel the fruit and cut them into chunks. Stick the chunks on long wooden skewers or cocktail sticks. Arrange the chunks in a colourful order. It is important that you prepare your fruits at the last minute before a meal, otherwise they will turn brown in the air. The appearance and taste of the fruit will be improved if you sprinkle them with a little lemon juice.

5 Make a model Negrito hut

Make a model Negrito hut like the one in the picture on page 30.

Roll out some plasticine or clay into a flat sheet. Stick thin twigs in it as shown in the picture below. Tie the twigs together at the top corners. Thatch the hut with dried grass, leaves or strips of paper.

If you can get permission, make a large Negrito hut in the garden or on the school field.

6 A world without money

Most of the natives of the tropical forests of the Amazon basin, the Congo and Malaysia have never seen money. They would not know what money was if they saw some, or know what to do with it. Imagine you lived in a part of the world where there was no money. Write a story describing what you would do. Say how you would get your clothes, food, and the other things you need to live.

7 Write a play

Write a short play about a day in the life of one of the tropical forest tribes. Ask your friends to help you to perform your play.

8 Latex

Pick a dandelion leaf or flower. You will notice that a milky-white liquid comes out of the broken stem. This is latex. It is very similar to the latex which comes from rubber trees. During the Second World War the Russians made a lot of their rubber tyres from dandelion latex.

Can you find any other plants which contain latex?

9 Mineral salts

Mineral salts are very important in the growth of all plants. They are particularly important to tropical forest plants. As we have seen, when tropical forests are cleared, the mineral salts are soon lost from the soil. The soil no longer grows good crops.

You can see these mineral salts if you put a handful of soil in a clean glass jar which has a lid to it. Half fill the jar with tap water. Put the lid on the jar and shake it.

Take a circular filter paper, or cut a circle from blotting paper. Fold the paper into a cone.

Moisten the inside of the funnel with water and place the cone of paper inside it. Stand the funnel over another clean jar and slowly and carefully pour your sample of water into the paper. The paper sieves out, or filters, the pieces of soil which are in the water. The water which drips out of the bottom of the filter paper looks perfectly clean.

Put some of this water in a clean saucer. Leave the saucer of water near a radiator or on a sunny windowsill. The water will evaporate and you will see a smear of mineral salts left around the saucer. What colour are they? Compare different samples of soil. Which contains most mineral salts?

10 A bottle garden

A bottle garden imitates, in miniature, the warm, moist conditions in a tropical forest.

You will need a large bottle made of clear glass. A sweet jar, laid on its side, also makes a good bottle garden.

Put a layer of washed gravel, about 5 centimetres deep, in the bottom of the bottle. A cardboard packing tube and a large funnel will help you to get the gravel to the bottom of the bottle without dirtying the sides.

If you can get some, next put in the bottle a layer of crushed charcoal about 5 centimetres deep. This helps to keep the inside of the bottle clean and fresh.

Finally add a layer of soil or potting compost 10 centimetres deep.

Use a spoon or an old table fork tied to a stick to dig holes for your plants. Mosses and small ferns grow well in a bottle garden, so do ivies, spider plants and African violets. Place the taller plants in the middle or at the back of the bottle.

Firm the plants down with a cotton reel fixed on a stick.

Trickle water gently down the sides of the bottle. Do not stand the bottle in direct sunlight. Keep a stopper on the bottle, but take it off for a while if the inside of the bottle starts to become clouded with condensation.

Things to find out

1 Draw or trace an outline map of the world. Shade in the areas of tropical forests. Mark in any large rivers which flow through the forests. Find out more about these rivers.

2 Natives in one of the tropical forests could probably obtain all the food they wanted with a bow and arrow. And yet people from somewhere else in the world would probably starve, even if they had a gun. Why do you think this would be?

3 The tropical forests near the West African coast used to be called 'the white man's grave'. Find out why this was.

4 One of the biggest dangers to the pygmies of the African tropical forests and the Amazon Indians is disease. Hundreds of these forest people have died because they caught diseases such as colds, influenza and measles brought to their part of the world by white people. Can you find out why these diseases should be so serious to the forest people when often they cause only mild illness in white people?

5 At one time most of the workers on plantations were slaves Find out where these slaves came from and how they were treated.

6 When tyres and other things are being made from rubber the rubber is usually vulcanised. What is vulcanisation? Why is it done? Where has the name vulcanisation come from?

7 What turns coffee beans from a green to a dark brown colour?

8 Rice is an important food crop which is grown in several tropical forest areas. Find out where rice is grown and how it is looked after. How does the mud carried by rivers help rice to grow?

9 Find out more about the tropical forest animals which are in danger of becoming extinct. What, if anything, is being done to save these animals?

10 A number of organisations, such as the *World Wildlife Fund* and the *Earthlife Foundation* are very worried about the loss of the world's tropical forests. Find out why these organisations are worried and what they are trying to do to reduce the loss of tropical forests.

For further information about **World Wide Fund for Nature** membership, please write to: **World Wide Fund for Nature, Panda House, Weyside Park, Godalming, Surrey GU7 1XR.**

For details of the **Rain Forest Campaign** contact: **Earthlife, 10 Belgrave Square, London SW1X 8PH.**

11 How do trees and other plants affect the air? Why are trees often planted by the sides of roads in towns?

Glossary

Here are the meanings of some words which you might have met for the first time in this book.

Buttress roots: roots which come from the trunk of a tree above ground and which support the tree like the guy-ropes on a tent.

Chlorophyll: the green substance which gives plants their colouring, and with which they trap sunlight to help make their food.

Crown: the name given to the part of a tree above the trunk. The crown is made up of branches, twigs and leaves.

Decay: to rot away.

Deciduous trees: trees which lose their leaves in the autumn and grow new ones the following spring.

Epiphyte: a plant which grows on another plant, using it for support so that it can reach the light.

Evaporate: when water is heated it disappears into the air as water vapour. We say the water has evaporated.

Evergreen trees: trees which do not lose all their leaves in the autumn but, instead, lose them a few at a time throughout the year.

Fertile: a good soil which is capable of growing many crops is said to be fertile.

Invertebrate animals: animals which do not have a backbone inside their bodies. Most invertebrates are quite small.

Jungle: a term sometimes used for waste ground which is not cultivated. Sometimes tropical forests are called jungles.

Latex: the milky-white juice inside rubber trees, from which rubber is made.

Lianes: woody climbing plants which grow in tropical forests.

Mineral salts: the chemical substances which trees and other plants obtain from the soil and use as food.

Parasites: plants or animals which obtain their food by living inside or on other plants or animals.

Plantations: forests which have been planted by people to produce crops which are sold.

Pygmies: the name given to tribes of very small people.

Rainforest: another name for evergreen tropical forests which grow in wet places.

Shifting cultivation: a type of farming in which people clear a piece of land and grow crops on it for a few years until the soil is no longer fertile. The people then move on to a new piece of land.

Timber: the name given to the wood of a tree.

Tropical forest: a forest which grows near to or on the Equator.

Water vapour: the invisible gas which is formed when water is heated.

Index